Samuel French Acting Edition

When We Wake Up Dead

by Dennis A. Allen II

‖SAMUEL FRENCH‖

Copyright © 2021 by Dennis A. Allen II
All Rights Reserved

WHEN WE WAKE UP DEAD is fully protected under the copyright laws of the United States of America, the British Commonwealth, including Canada, and all member countries of the Berne Convention for the Protection of Literary and Artistic Works, the Universal Copyright Convention, and/or the World Trade Organization conforming to the Agreement on Trade Related Aspects of Intellectual Property Rights. All rights, including professional and amateur stage productions, recitation, lecturing, public reading, motion picture, radio broadcasting, television, online/digital production, and the rights of translation into foreign languages are strictly reserved.

ISBN 978-0-573-70902-9

www.concordtheatricals.com
www.concordtheatricals.co.uk

FOR PRODUCTION INQUIRIES

UNITED STATES AND CANADA
info@concordtheatricals.com
1-866-979-0447

UNITED KINGDOM AND EUROPE
licensing@concordtheatricals.co.uk
020-7054-7200

Each title is subject to availability from Concord Theatricals Corp., depending upon country of performance. Please be aware that *WHEN WE WAKE UP DEAD* may not be licensed by Concord Theatricals Corp. in your territory. Professional and amateur producers should contact the nearest Concord Theatricals Corp. office or licensing partner to verify availability.

CAUTION: Professional and amateur producers are hereby warned that *WHEN WE WAKE UP DEAD* is subject to a licensing fee. The purchase, renting, lending or use of this book does not constitute a license to perform this title(s), which license must be obtained from Concord Theatricals Corp. prior to any performance. Performance of this title(s) without a license is a violation of federal law and may subject the producer and/or presenter of such performances to civil penalties. Both amateurs and professionals considering a production are strongly advised to apply to the appropriate agent before starting rehearsals, advertising, or booking a theatre. A licensing fee must be paid whether the title(s) is presented for charity or gain and whether or not admission is charged. Professional/Stock licensing fees are quoted upon application to Concord Theatricals Corp.

This work is published by Samuel French, an imprint of Concord Theatricals Corp.

No one shall make any changes in this title(s) for the purpose of production. No part of this book may be reproduced, stored in a retrieval system, scanned, uploaded, or transmitted in any form, by any means, now known or yet to be invented, including mechanical, electronic, digital, photocopying, recording, videotaping, or otherwise, without the prior written permission of the publisher. No one shall share this title(s), or any part of this title(s), through any social media or file hosting websites.

For all inquiries regarding motion picture, television, online/digital and other media rights, please contact Concord Theatricals Corp.

MUSIC AND THIRD-PARTY MATERIALS USE NOTE

Licensees are solely responsible for obtaining formal written permission from copyright owners to use copyrighted music and/or other copyrighted third-party materials (e.g., artworks, logos) in the performance of this play and are strongly cautioned to do so. If no such permission is obtained by the licensee, then the licensee must use only original music and materials that the licensee owns and controls. Licensees are solely responsible and liable for clearances of all third-party copyrighted materials, including without limitation music, and shall indemnify the copyright owners of the play(s) and their licensing agent, Concord Theatricals Corp., against any costs, expenses, losses and liabilities arising from the use of such copyrighted third-party materials by licensees. For music, please contact the appropriate music licensing authority in your territory for the rights to any incidental music.

IMPORTANT BILLING AND CREDIT REQUIREMENTS

If you have obtained performance rights to this title, please refer to your licensing agreement for important billing and credit requirements.

WHEN WE WAKE UP DEAD was first produced at the New Workshop Theatre at Brooklyn College in March of 2016. The production was directed by Christopher Burris, with set design by Pei-Wen Huang-Shea, costume design by Sabrina Bianca Guillaume, lighting design by Byungchul Lee, music and sound design by Mark Bruckner, and fight direction by Robert Tuftee. The stage manager was Eddy Roland. The cast was as follows:

BRYANT WALKER . . . . .Lorenzo Cromwell
JAMES WALKER . . . . .Chakeefe Gordon
EMORY HILL . . . . .Shomari Pinnock
UNCLE CECIL. . . . . .Michael Gaines
AUNT CHERYL. . . . . .Jacqueline Springfield
LYNN . . . . Kristin Fulton

CHARACTERS

BRYANT WALKER – 19, James' fraternal twin, NY

JAMES WALKER – 19, Bryant's fraternal twin, came out of the womb first, NY

EMORY HILL – 17, Bryant and James' cousin, MS

UNCLE CECIL – 60, Emory's father, Cheryl's husband of twenty years, MS

AUNT CHERYL – 41, Emory's mother, Bryant and James' maternal aunt, MS by way of MI

LYNN – 37, Cheryl's younger sister, Bryant and James' mother

SETTING

Somewhere, MS

TIME

The Present

AUTHOR'S NOTES

A breath: not to be taken literally – or maybe it is – inhale or exhale or both.

A moment: more of an emotional shift than a time indication – some moments take more time than others.

A minute: pause long enough to cause discomfort.

Double slashes (//) cut off and overlap dialogue.

Parentheses ( ) indicate a whisper or an aside.

Place: The stage should be sectioned into three rooms. The front room holds the kitchen and the living room and has the only door to outside. The middle room is Cecil and Cheryl's bedroom. The back room is Emory's bedroom. The middle and back rooms are reached by traveling a long hallway; the wall should be translucent so that the silhouettes of the bodies can be seen traveling from room to room. The entire space is a mix of antique and modern furniture and art. The back room is completely stark except for a bed, a tub basin, and a dresser drawer.

PROLOGUE

(A dim amber light fills the middle room, revealing a chair with a noose hanging above it. **EMORY** *enters; his face is hidden by shadow. He immediately steps up onto the chair, puts his head through the noose, and tightens it on his neck...)*

CECIL. "Well, what else could we do? He was hopeless. I'm no bully; I never hurt a nigger in my life. I like niggers – in their place – I know how to work 'em. But I just decided it was time a few people got put on notice. As long as I live and can do anything about it, niggers are gonna stay in their place. Niggers ain't gonna vote where I live. If they did, they'd control the government. They ain't gonna go to school with my kids. And when a nigger gets close to mentioning sex with a white woman, he's tired o' livin'. I'm likely to kill him. Me and my folks fought for this country, and we got some rights. I stood there in that shed and listened to that nigger throw that poison at me, and I just made up my mind. 'Chicago boy,' I said, 'I'm tired of 'em sending your kind down here to stir up trouble. Goddam you, I'm going to make an example of you – just so everybody can know how me and my folks stand.'"

See that, printed in 1956 a year after they got acquitted. No shame. Those "men" did some horrible things to that boy before they killed him. And Emmett refused to apologize; they tortured him, threatened to kill him and Emmett would not give them what they wanted. These fools were doing God's work and didn't even know it. God uses us to carry out his ultimate plan.

They thought they was doing what they had to do to keep things the way they were but killing Emmett way they did led to his mama leaving the casket open for the world to see and that was the thing that Ms. Rosa Parks was thinking about when she decided not to give up her seat, most folk don't know that fact. As horrible a thing as his death was it's directly connected to sparking the civil rights movement. It's always death, always death that brings about change in the world. If you can have a say in it, die for something die for a cause, now of course Emmett didn't know he was dying for a cause and really most never do. But if you can have a say...

(CHERYL's voice from somewhere offstage:)

CHERYL. Cecil! Let them boys get some sleep it's late and I don't want them nodding off in church tomorrow!

CECIL. Alright my Love, alright. Go to sleep.

PART I

I.

(**EMORY** *steps off the chair. His body flails and convulses as it instinctively clings to life. He kicks over the chair.*)

(*A light change. A breath.*)

(*The room pulsates with the low lub-dub of a heartbeat. A tinny, high-pitched tone [like the ringing sound that torments ears after they've been exposed to abusively loud sounds] swells and fills the room. As the high-pitched tone swells, the lights brighten simultaneously. Noises fill the room [birds, crickets, dogs barking, people arguing, a truck's engine, metal springs of a screen door cry out, the slamming of a door].*)

(*Normalcy.*)

(**JAMES** *has entered the home. He is carrying a duffle bag and pulling a small luggage bag on wheels. He wears sunglasses, a white short-sleeved polo shirt, plaid shorts, Nike Air Max that perfectly match the color scheme of the shorts, and a Fossil watch with a dial color that also perfectly matches the ensemble.* **BRYANT** *yells at him from outside:*)

BRYANT. Oh so you just gonna let the door slam in my face!

JAMES. Shut up.

Aunt Cheryl! Uncle Cecil?!

You home?!

BRYANT. Some country nigger shit always leaving the door open...

(He enters.)

(The screen door cries out and slams.)

*(**BRYANT** wears a du-rag, tank top, jeans, fresh [new] pair of Timberland boots, and bead and/or shell-style bracelets on his wrists.)*

I expected Uncle Cecil to be on the porch to greet us, sitting in a rocking chair chewin' on some tobaccy, holding a shotgun.

Damn it's hot!

JAMES. Hello?! Emory?! Aunt Cheryl?

Maybe they're at the hospital.

BRYANT. No wonder racism ran rampant down here, it's slavery hot!

*(**JAMES** walks to the back room and sees **EMORY** hanging. **JAMES** doesn't move. He watches the body swing.)*

Jay man, we gonna have to buy them AC, this is stupid. I feel like bustin' out into an old negro spiritual, just,

"WADE IN THE WAAATA WAAAAADE IN THA WATA CHILDREN WAAA..."

*(He enters the back room. He sees **EMORY** and rushes to his body.)*

Oh my God. Oh my God.

(He wraps his arms around **EMORY**'s *legs and lifts him.)*

Jay help me! Shit Emory man hold on. Jay!

JAMES. He obviously wants to die, just let him.

BRYANT. JAMES! Please... Emory hold on dawg I got you. I got you.

*(***JAMES*** walks over to the chair, picks it up, and places it next to* **BRYANT.** *He gets up on the chair and attempts to loosen the noose.)*

JAMES. Hold him higher. Hold still.

BRYANT. I'm trying man hurry up. Em we got you cuz just please hang in there.

JAMES. Ha.

BRYANT. Jay?!

JAMES. I can't get his neck out.

BRYANT. Cut the rope, do something! Jay!!

JAMES. All right, stop yelling at me!

(He goes to his bag and takes out a folding pocket knife. He stands on the chair and cuts the rope.)

*(***BRYANT*** holds and guides* **EMORY**'s *body gently to the ground.* **BRYANT** *takes the rope from around* **EMORY**'s *neck and throws it across the room.)*

BRYANT. Em? EM? I think...

Yeah he's still breathing.

Shit.

JAMES. Well that was exciting.

BRYANT. Yo. You. Are.

What's up with you?

JAMES. What? Come on B, don't look at me like that.

BRYANT. You were just standing there. Like standing there.

JAMES. I was in shock.

BRYANT. Shock. You weren't in no damn shock.

(A moment.)

We came just in time.

JAMES. He's not going to see it like that.

What?

He's not.

This is like the third time, the brother obviously has an agenda...

BRYANT. Stop.

JAMES. How many times have we heard Mom buggin' on the phone, comforting Aunt Cheryl over ignorant ass, crazy ass Emory.

BRYANT. Yo I'm not even entertainin' you right now.

*(He turns his attention to **EMORY**.)*

JAMES. B. you know I'm right. He's just going to try it again.

Waste.

BRYANT. Emory can you hear me? Yo?

I think we should call 911 to be safe.

JAMES. You think they got fast responders out here?

We'd be better off taking him ourselves.

BRYANT. Maybe we should take him.

JAMES. His heart's beating, he's breathing, he's fine.

BRYANT. I don't know.

JAMES. Do you even know how to get to the hospital?

BRYANT. Ah, we could just use...

JAMES. On the way here the GPS told me to make a right into the river.

He's fine.

BRYANT. Should we at least move him to the bed?

JAMES. No, just leave him there till he comes to.

Safer not to move him.

BRYANT. Yo this is crazy.

JAMES. It was your idea to come down and visit.

BRYANT. Uncle C might not be around much longer yo.

JAMES. Apparently neither will Emory.

BRYANT. Come on Jay, damn.

Shit, it's hot...

You know what I thought when I saw him hanging from that rope?

JAMES. Yeah.

"Hang in there."

(Laughs.)

You actually told him to hang in there.

BRYANT. *(Chuckles.)* It's not funny.

JAMES. That's a lie.

It's funny as hell.

"Come on cuz, hang in there."

BRYANT. I was panicking.

Shut up.

JAMES. Hang. In. There?

Ha!

BRYANT. First thing I thought was,

"Damn it's so racist niggas are hanging themselves out here."

JAMES. What?!

Does Aunt Cheryl have a cell phone?

BRYANT. Not that I know of.

Em?! Emory!

Shit it's hot.

JAMES. *(Chuckles.)* You think that's why he keeps trying?

BRYANT. 'Cause it's hot?!

For Real, for real we just got here and death IS looking like a good look...

Ooo! I bet Aunt Cheryl has a pitcher of her iced tea in the fridge.

JAMES. Pour me a glass.

>   *(**BRYANT** gets up, goes to the front room, and walks directly to the refrigerator. **JAMES** stares at **EMORY**. **BRYANT** opens the fridge and pulls out a large pitcher.)*

BRYANT. Bingo nigga!

>   *(He looks around and then starts to drink directly out of the pitcher.)*

JAMES. WE don't commit suicide you weak-willed bitch.

You're an embarrassment.

To the race.

To the family.

Waste.

>(**BRYANT** *lets out a guttural sound of satisfaction:*)

BRYANT. Ooooooooooo... Ahhhhhh...

Shit.

I think I just got diabetes but damn it was worth it!

>(*He puts the pitcher back into the fridge and walks into the back room.*)

Should we be worried he hasn't woken up yet?

JAMES. Huh?

Oh no, he's fine. He's fine.

Where's my iced tea?

BRYANT. In the pitcher in the fridge. It's good too, yo.

JAMES. I said pour me a glass, man.

BRYANT. I got you next time.

I promise.

JAMES. Tssh, yeah.

>(*He walks to the fridge.*)

BRYANT. (Damn cuzzo, this is not a good look. If I knew you were hurting like this we woulda flew you to NY baby. You know?)

Em? Em?

>(**JAMES** *retrieves a glass from the drying rack, gets out the iced tea, and pours himself a glass. He takes a sip.*)

JAMES. Whew! Damn.

BRYANT. It's good right?! Just like when we were young.

> (**JAMES** *pours the rest of his tea out in the sink.*)

JAMES. Yeah, It's yummy.

> (*He looks outside. The sound of a vehicle's engine and tires on a gravel road.*)

Aunt Cheryl just pulled up!

Drama time.

BRYANT. Damn Emory, you really tryin' to break this woman's heart my dude.

JAMES. B? You hear me?! B?! Aunt Cheryl's here!

> (**BRYANT** *joins* **JAMES** *in the front room.*)

BRYANT. Okay, I'm going to...

JAMES. We shouldn't tell her.

BRYANT. What?

JAMES. She's been burdened with a ton of stress lately. We shouldn't say anything.

BRYANT. He's laid out on the floor back there...

JAMES. Just trust me. For all she knows he fell asleep in a weird spot.

BRYANT. What?! Bro...

JAMES. Just act normal.

BRYANT. Come on man! Why'd you say that? You know I can't ever act normal when you tell me to act normal.

JAMES. Just chill...

> (*The screen door cries out.*)

BRYANT.   **JAMES.**

Hey, hey hey! Aunt Cheryl!   Hi, Aunt Cheryl.

CHERYL. Why are y'all standing there looking shady?

> (**BRYANT** *explodes into nervous, insincere laughter.* **JAMES** *shoots him a look.*)

BRYANT. Aunt Cheryl you crazy you stay crazy.

CHERYL. Uh-huh. Y'all just gonna stand there or are you going to help me with these groceries?

EMORY!

BRYANT. We got you Aunt Cheryl we got you.

> (**JAMES** *holds the door open.* **BRYANT** *goes to take the bags from* **CHERYL.**)

CHERYL. I got these. There are some more bags in the back seat. Thank you baby.

> (**BRYANT** *exits out to get the rest of the groceries.* **JAMES** *continues holding open the door.* **CHERYL** *unpacks the bags in the kitchen.*)

You must've just got here, I wasn't at the store for that long. I need to head right back out, they're releasing your uncle this afternoon. Emory!

JAMES. Uncle Cecil is done with his treatment?

CHERYL. No. He's decided to come home.

JAMES. Oh. // But?

CHERYL. You just gonna hold the door open, letting the flies in and not help your brother?

JAMES. I am helping by holding the door open.

CHERYL. You always did find a way to make him do all the dirty work, why should it be different now? EMORY BOY YOU BETTER NOT STILL BE SLEEP!

JAMES. Aunt Cheryl why is Uncle...

(**BRYANT** *enters, struggling to carry way too many bags.*)

CHERYL. What in the world is wrong with,

James help your brother...

JAMES. I'm holding the door –

BRYANT. I got it –

CHERYL. Bryant, child you're going to break something –

BRYANT. Nah, I'm good –

(*He gets inside, realizes he is going to drop the bags, so he falls backwards onto his butt to save the contents of the bags.* **CHERYL** *shrieks.* **JAMES** *laughs. The screen door slams.* **EMORY** *enters.*)

EMORY. All this noise could wake the dead.

CHERYL. Apparently...

JAMES. Pssh!

CHERYL. ...Come help your fool cousin with these bags please. Should be ashamed of yourself sleeping past noon. Come on, sloth is a deadly sin you know.

EMORY. Yes ma'am.

(**CHERYL** *kisses* **JAMES** *and* **BRYANT** *on their foreheads.*)

CHERYL. It's good to see you two, I'm so glad you decided to visit. Y'all go ahead and put the food away for me, I'm going to pick up Cecil. You two will be sleeping on the air mattress in the living room, Cecil is staying in Emory's room, Bubba put your clothes in the top two drawers in my dresser and whatever else you use regularly I don't want you having to go into your room for something every second disturbing your father. I made some tea and there are turkey sandwiches in there, help yourselves. I should only be an hour or so. When I get back I'll start on dinner. I want that room clean before I come home with your father, you hear me?

EMORY. Yes ma'am.

CHERYL. And you mind your cousins, they're in charge while I'm gone.

EMORY. Yes ma'am.

CHERYL. Well, listen to James; Bryant ain't got no sense.

BRYANT. Hey!

> (**CHERYL** *exits. The screen door cries.* **JAMES** *catches it before it slams. A minute. The sound of a vehicle's engine and tires on a gravel road.* **EMORY** *starts putting the groceries away.*)

EMORY. Hey y'all.

BRYANT. "Hey y'all." ...Hey? Y'all? That's what you say?

EMORY. You like "Hi" betta?

BRYANT. Nigga is you crazy?!

JAMES. You have to ask that?

EMORY. Could you help me put these away please?

> (**BRYANT** *helps* **EMORY**. **JAMES** *watches.*)

BRYANT. Em, my dude. I love you like my little brother. You know that. Why are you trying to off yourself?

> *(A moment.)*

Are you off your meds?

JAMES. More like off his rocker.

BRYANT. Yo, are you going to help us?

JAMES. Nope.

(He walks to the back room to get his bags.)

EMORY. James's the same I see.

BRYANT. Yeah well he's James. Hey. Hey? You stop taking your medication?

EMORY. No.

BRYANT. Are you lying?

EMORY. I ain't lyin'.

BRYANT. So what's good man?

EMORY. Nothing.

BRYANT. You sad about your pops?

EMORY. Daddy's been dying a long time now.

BRYANT. What's that mean?

EMORY. I'm fine cuz.

BRYANT. Don't give me fine. You are not fine. Fine is not bungee jumping with your neck. As matter of fact if you look up fine in the dictionary it says, "the opposite of bungee jumping with your neck."

(JAMES enters.)

JAMES. Leave him alone.

BRYANT. What, like you tried to?

JAMES. Bubba obviously has his reasons. You badgering him won't make things magically better. Leave him alone.

(EMORY finishes with the groceries and walks to the back room to move his stuff to his parents' room.)

BRYANT. Why you so cold-hearted?

JAMES. You got all the warm and fuzzy genes.

BRYANT. I'm serious. You stay walking around like you don't give a fuck, but I know you do.

JAMES. I'm not cold-hearted, I'm logical. Logic you should try it sometime.

BRYANT. *(Mockingly.)* Oh "logic you should try it sometime."

JAMES. Yeah like not carrying 100 bags at once

BRYANT. If you would've helped me and not stand there like a worthless doorman...

JAMES. Two trips. That would have been logical. Making two trips.

BRYANT. Why when I could do it in one. It's hot as hell don't nobody want to go back and forth outside in that sun.

JAMES. You are borderline retarded.

> (**EMORY** *sees the cut rope on the floor and puts it in Cheryl's dresser with the rest of his clothes.*)

BRYANT. You're an all the way sociopath, just gonna let your little cousin hang himself.

JAMES. Rational thought. Logic. Something your monkey ass is missing.

BRYANT. Baby Dahmer over here. Imma start calling you baby Dahmer.

JAMES. I'm not crazy.

BRYANT. Next thing I know you're going to start eating motherfuckers and putting half-ate asses in the fridge.

JAMES. I'm not crazy you dumb shit. I didn't put the rope around his neck.

BRYANT. Then I gotta explain to the cops why there's frozen half-asses in the crib. Be on the news, the neighbors on some, "He was such a good kid I would have never thought."

JAMES. Emory is crazy. Not me. I just know you can't save everybody.

BRYANT. And you black so the whole community gonna be pissed 'cause only crazy white folk do that shit. Eatin' asses. And niggas gonna look at me funny 'cause we twins. And my sex life gonna go down the tubes 'cause chicks are gonna think I'm like your nutty ass.

*(**EMORY** finishes moving his things to his parents' room and enters the front room.)*

JAMES. I'm not crazy! He's crazy! Him! He's the one on drugs. Trying to kill his self every other month. One day he's fine the next day his unstable ass is on a bridge somewhere. Crazy worthless nigger.

EMORY. I missed you too Jay.

(He exits. The screen door cries out and slams.)

BRYANT. Hashtag my brother's an asshole.

JAMES. Shut up.

BRYANT. Go apologize.

JAMES. What for?

BRYANT. Come on.

JAMES. It wasn't even directed towards him I was mad at your annoying ass.

BRYANT. Don't tell me.

JAMES. Whatever.

*(A moment. The screen door cries out. **JAMES** exits. The door slams.)*

BRYANT. Tea and turkey time.

Damn it's hot.

> *(He goes to the fridge. A light change. A breath.)*

II.

> (**BRYANT** *stands in front of the fridge, holding the door open.* **CHERYL**, **JAMES**, *and* **CECIL** *are in the back room.* **CECIL** *lies asleep in the bed.* **EMORY** *sits on the floor of the middle room with headphones on his ears, writing in a marble notebook.*)

JAMES. Here look, what if I showed him the knife he gave me?

CHERYL. Maybe. Let him rest.

JAMES. He didn't recognize me.

CHERYL. No, he's just weak is all. Never liked hospitals and doesn't trust doctors, so didn't get any real sleep.

JAMES. It's been like four years, do you think that's why he didn't know me?

CHERYL. He's tired baby. Just tired. He's seen the pictures your mother sends. He knows you. Let him rest. You can talk to him later. Come on I'm going to start dinner.

> (**CHERYL** *and* **JAMES** *walk to the front room.* **CHERYL** *sticks her head into the middle room.*)

Bubba your father is sleeping, don't disturb him.

(She doesn't wait for an acknowledgement.)

Unless you plan on replacing every piece of food in there and paying my electric bill I'm gonna need you to get your head out my icebox now.

BRYANT. I'm sorry Aunt Cheryl it's just so hot. How'd Uncle C get you from Michigan to Mississippi?

CHERYL. Love will make you do things you'd never dream.

BRYANT. His pimp game was strong.

CHERYL. Excuse me?

BRYANT. It's okay Aunt Cheryl, we grown now.

JAMES. I'm grown now. I don't now what he is.

BRYANT. We know Uncle C was a straight up Pimp.

CHERYL. And what I'm his Ho?

JAMES. Uh-oh.

BRYANT. No no no no no no no no that's not what I'm saying.

JAMES. Back Ped-dle!! Reverse. Beep. Beep. Beep. Beep.

BRYANT. Hush! No, wait not a pimp in the traditional sense of the word. I'm saying he had to be smooth as hell to bag you.

CHERYL. Bag?

BRYANT. And he's like twenty years older.

CHERYL. How do you know he "bagged" me and it wasn't me that "bagged" him?

JAMES. Oh! It's big pimpin' baby.

*(He starts to beatbox and make trumpet sounds with his mouth. **BRYANT** joins in, dancing and playfully rapping to **JAMES'** beat. **CHERYL** is amused and entertained for a moment. Meanwhile, **EMORY** gets up, walks to the back room, watches his father sleep, and writes in the notebook. **CHERYL** stops enjoying the twins' performance. **BRYANT** notices and gets **JAMES'** attention.)*

(A moment.)

BRYANT. Uncle Cecil's going to be fine Aunt Cheryl. Right Jay? Right?

JAMES. Yeah. Yeah he's the strongest man I've ever met.

BRYANT. Word. You remember that time he saved me from that Rottweiler? I ain't never seen a man punch a dog, let alone knock it out.

CHERYL. I remember that day. It was your fault messing with the Robertsons' //...

JAMES. He wouldn't have needed saving if he just stuck to the plan.

BRYANT. What?!

JAMES. All you had to do was grab the dog's bowl, run and climb the tree.

BRYANT. Yo if I stopped to climb the tree I would've had a hole in my ass to this day.

CHERYL. Why were you messing with that dog in the first place?

BRYANT. Jay Dub over there bet me twenty dollars I couldn't steal the dog's bowl.

CHERYL. You always let your brother get you into trouble.

BRYANT. I ran past the tree screaming my face off. Uncle Cecil came out the house with his big southern black buck swag, snatched the dog by the collar with one hand and molly-whopped him with the other.

CHERYL. Where was my son during all of this?

BRYANT. Up in the tree with Jay Dub.

CHERYL. Lord.

Is that the same day you broke your arm James?

JAMES. Yeah. Emory's ass pushed me out of the tree.

CHERYL. What?! No one ever told me that's what happened.

BRYANT. We didn't want him to get in trouble. Tell her why. Tell her why he pushed you.

JAMES. He kept telling me to go save Bryant from the dog and I was like, "No." So he pushed me.

CHERYL. Oh my god. Six years later your mother still hasn't forgiven me. Sent one son home with a fear of dogs and the other with a broken arm. Lord Jesus.

BRYANT. I'm not scared of dogs.

I'm suspicious. There's a difference.

CHERYL. Both of you are a mess. I'm going to get dinner started, go keep your cousin company.

BRYANT. Has he been okay?

CHERYL. Bubba's been fine. As good as a son can be when his father's...

Sick.

BRYANT. He's been staying on his meds and all that?

CHERYL. Yes. Why? What would make you...

JAMES. Nothing.

BRYANT. Yeah. Nothing.

CHERYL. Well go on now, get. You know I don't like folk floating around while I'm cooking.

> (**EMORY** *moves back to the middle room and sits on the floor.* **JAMES** *and* **BRYANT** *enter the middle room.* **CHERYL** *begins preparing a meal.* **CECIL** *stirs in his sleep.*)

BRYANT. What you listening to cuzzo? Em? Yo!

> (**JAMES** *snatches* **EMORY**'s *headphones off.*)

EMORY. Just some instrumentals.

BRYANT. You still writin'? Let me hear something –

EMORY. No. Don't really feel like it.

JAMES. Come on, go ahead, kick that bipolar flow.

BRYANT. I can't wait till he blacks out and beats the shit outta you.

JAMES. Pssh. Yeah okay. That day never cometh.

BRYANT. Please Bubba?

Peep, we've been dancin' around what happened earlier today. We don't ever have to speak on it, if you spit something right now. But it has to be right now.

JAMES. Yeah Bub. Kick that seven-thirty flow. Your rap name should be Bub-seven-thirty.

BRYANT. Asshole. Bub, come on man, lemme hear something.

EMORY. You're not gonna leave me alone until I do, are you?

BRYANT. You so smat. And kind. And impotant.

EMORY. Death. Heaven and Hell.

> (**JAMES** *sucks his teeth.* **BRYANT** *encourages* **EMORY** *to continue. A transition. During* **EMORY**'s *rap,* **CECIL**'s *stirring increases.* **CHERYL** *silently cries.* **JAMES** *moves to the front room.* **BRYANT** *moves to the back room.* **EMORY** *goes to the bed; by his last line he is lying down in the bed.*)

DEATH. HEAVEN AND HELL.
WHAT ORDER DO THEY COME I COULD NEVER TELL.
WHO WOULD YOU BLAME IF LUCIFER NEVER FELL?
HOW WOULD YOU SUCCEED WITH NO SOUL TO SELL?
WHAT GOOD DOES THE TOLLS WHEN I CAN'T HEAR THE BELL?
CAN'T HEAR THE BELL.
DEATH. HEAVEN AND HELL.
YOU'RE DEAD WAY LONGER THAN YOU'RE EVER ALIVE.
IF HEAVEN'S SO GOOD WHY STRUGGLE TO SURVIVE?

FOCUS ON THE FORM WHENEVER TAKING A DIVE.
I'M TAKING THE DIVE.
DEATH. HEAVEN AND HELL.
WITH NO GOD HOW DO YOU DETERMINE A SIN?
WITH NO GAME HOW DO YOU DETERMINE A WIN?
WITH NO FINISH WHERE THE HELL DO I BEGIN?
WHERE IN HELL DO I BEGIN?

(A breath. **CHERYL** *is in the front room inflating an air mattress.* **JAMES** *watches her.* **BRYANT** *stands in the back room.* **CECIL** *lies in the bed.* **EMORY** *sleeps.)*

BRYANT. He's really good Unc. I know you're not big into spoken word but Em is deep. He could actually make it. I hope you're around to see him make it. I hope he's around to see him make it. Bubba needs you Uncle C, you gotta get better. You don't look so good Unc, like you look bad for real. Man if you can survive living down here with this heat and you were around for Jim Crow and shit, pssh this cancer shit should be a piece of cake. James's still an asshole. Remember when you called him that last time. That shit was funny man, I ain't never heard a grown-up call a kid an asshole to his face. And you meant it too. "Little asshole." I've been calling him an asshole ever since. I think he likes it.

(He sees that **CECIL** *is awake.)*

Oh, hey, hey Uncle Cecil. Damn did I wake you? My fault. It's me Bryant. You good? You need anything.

*(***CECIL*** whispers.* **BRYANT** *gets closer so he can hear.)*

No it's me Bry, Emory's sleep I think...

You want some water? Hold on I got you.

(He walks to the front room. He peeks his head into the middle room, sees that **EMORY**

is sleeping, and continues to the front. **JAMES** *is making the bed.)*

*(***CHERYL** *watches.)*

BRYANT. Yo, Uncle C is awake, he wants some water.

JAMES. You woke him up?

BRYANT. No I didn't wake him up. He just woke up.

(He goes to the fridge, pulls out a container of water, and pours a glass. **CECIL** *attempts to get out of the bed and falls out. The thump startles* **CHERYL** *and wakes* **EMORY**. **JAMES**, **BRYANT**, *and* **CHERYL** *move to the back room.* **EMORY** *stays in the bed.)*

CHERYL. Sweet Jesus.

BRYANT. Damn. I told him I'd get it.

CHERYL. Cecil?

JAMES. What is that smell? Did he?

(He gags.)

BRYANT. Shit.

CHERYL. Watch your mouth.

BRYANT. Sorry.

CHERYL. Come help me get him up.

*(***BRYANT** *moves to help.* **JAMES** *stands still.)*

BRYANT. Jay? Come on dawg.

*(***JAMES** *leaves and goes to the middle room.)*

Bitchass...

CHERYL. Hey!

BRYANT. Sorry.

CHERYL. Help me get him up. Never mind. Never mind.

Go to the bathroom you'll see a small bucket on the floor and sponge inside. Fill the bucket halfway with warm water and a little soap, grab a towel, a washcloth and a garbage bag and bring 'em here.

> (**BRYANT** *exits to the bathroom.* **CHERYL** *strips* **CECIL** *naked.*)

EMORY. What happen?

> (*A moment.*)

JAMES. You're going to try again, aren't you?

EMORY. Leave me alone.

JAMES. I know you are. And I know you're lying about taking your pills.

EMORY. So?

JAMES. So you're a weak little punk that's doing nothing but making things harder around here for Aunt Cheryl.

EMORY. Leave me alone.

> (**BRYANT** *returns with the items.*)

CHERYL. Thank you angel, now grab me a diaper out of the small bin under the bed.

> (**CECIL** *moans in pain and protest.*)

I know baby but this is easier and less painful this way. We'll be done as quick as possible Love.

JAMES. I mean you're so damn selfish. If we didn't come when we did Aunt Cheryl would have found you swinging from the damn ceiling. Why would you do that to her? Go into the woods to off yourself not in the house that she lives.

EMORY. I'm not going to tell you again. Let me be.

JAMES. Or what? Huh? What?

CHERYL. Okay, good, let me just get…okay great.

> (**CHERYL** and **BRYANT** *continue to clean and dress* **CECIL**.)

JAMES. If you're gonna die. Die for a cause. Make your death of some use. Your life has been a waste so far.

EMORY. You're not my daddy, James.

> (**JAMES** *gets right into* **EMORY**'s *face.*)

JAMES. How are you Uncle Cecil's son? Huh? How? You know I always thought you were adopted

EMORY. Stop. I don't want to hurt you.

JAMES. Nigga please. You can't even effectively hurt yourself. Just admit that you don't really want to die. Everyone that ever really wanted to die, is dead. Your attempts are just a bitchass cry for attention.

EMORY. Leave me be.

JAMES. When you gonna stop acting crazy? Huh?

> (*He pokes* **EMORY** *in the chest.*)

Huh?

> (*Pokes him again.*)

EMORY. Stop.

JAMES. Stop acting!

> (**EMORY** *grabs* **JAMES** *by the shirt, drives him into the wall, and then throws him to the floor. The thump startles* **CHERYL**.)

CHERYL. God what now? I can finish up here. Go see what your brother and cousin are doing please.

(**BRYANT** *moves to the middle room.* **EMORY** *is on top of* **JAMES** *and has him pinned to the floor.*)

JAMES. Get off me.

BRYANT. I knew this day would come.

JAMES. Get him off me.

BRYANT. Nope.

EMORY. I don't care what you think about me, what you say; but don't touch me.

BRYANT. Yeah! Don't touch him.

JAMES. Get off!

BRYANT. You know if this was jail you'd be getting piped right now? He'd have you washing his drawers and everything.

(**EMORY** *stands up and walks out to the front.* **JAMES** *stays on the floor.* **BRYANT** *follows* **EMORY**. **CHERYL** *lies in the bed with* **CECIL**.)

Cuz. Emory. hold on man.

(**EMORY** *stops.*)

Don't let Jay get to you.

EMORY. I'm fine.

BRYANT. Yeah. Right. You can talk to me you know.

EMORY. About what?

BRYANT. About anything. Everything. Look I just saw Uncle Cecil's bare ass and penis, I think I need someone to talk to. Mom said Uncle C probably didn't have much longer but I didn't know what to expect when I got here. You know what I'm sayin'. I definitely didn't expect to see him ass naked covered in shit. Or you, hanging by your neck. I don't know how much more I can take.

EMORY. You be all right.

BRYANT. Huh?

EMORY. Said you strong. You'll be just fine.

BRYANT. I am kinda diesel huh?

(He does a series of bodybuilder poses.)

Damn Bub, you don't laugh no more. I mean you've always been an intense kid but I remember you used to laugh all the time.

EMORY. Don't feel much like smilin'.

BRYANT. Yeah I can dig it, but damn. You not even gonna smirk? I don't need your whole mouth just this cheek, this half right here, just a little, real quick you know? I mean it'll look like you got a bad tick or Tourette's but I'll know it's your half smile.

Okay guess not.

(He goes to the fridge and takes out the pitcher of iced tea.)

You want some?

No? Okay.

(He drinks a few gulps directly from the pitcher and then puts it back in the fridge. **JAMES** *stands up and starts shadowboxing, fighting an unseen opponent.* **CECIL** *and* **CHERYL** *are still.)*

EMORY. I stopped takin' my pills.

(A moment.)

BRYANT. Why?

EMORY. Felt like I was waking up dead.

BRYANT. What?

EMORY. Mom told me Daddy had six months tops to live and I didn't cry.

BRYANT. That's it? You didn't cry?

You stopped taking your pills because you didn't cry.

EMORY. I used to cry at everything. You know that.

BRYANT. So you not crying is now bad?

EMORY. It's the one time I should have cried. You should have seen the way Momma looked at me when she told me. She was crying her eyes out and I just watched her. Felt heartless. I even squinted up my face real tight to try and squeeze out a tear or two. Nothing. Daddy's gonna pass on. He gonna be… I'll be damned if I don't cry at his funeral. I won't have folk thinkin' I don't love my daddy.

BRYANT. So what was this morning about?

EMORY. What?

BRYANT. You tried to kill yourself. What's the deal with that?

EMORY. When?

BRYANT. This morning, Jay and I found you hanging. You don't remember that?

EMORY. No.

BRYANT. Emory man you need help. Maybe my mom can send a better prescription.

EMORY. I'm fine. Just wish I would stop dreaming about killing my father.

> *(He exits. The screen door cries out and slams.* **JAMES** *collapses from exhaustion.* **CHERYL** *pops up, startled.* **BRYANT** *falls onto the air mattress.)*

III.

*(A light change. **JAMES** moves to the front room. A moment. **BRYANT** and **JAMES** lie on the air mattress in the front room. **CECIL** and **CHERYL** lie on the bed in the back room.)*

BRYANT. Jay?

JAMES. Hmm?

BRYANT. You asleep?

JAMES. I hope so.

BRYANT. I just realized I haven't slept in almost two days.

JAMES. There's no time like the present.

BRYANT. Nah bro I can't sleep now. Not tired. And the sun's coming up. You know I can't sleep when the sun's up.

JAMES. Try something new.

BRYANT. Shit. Not tired. Where you think Emory is?

JAMES. Fuck him.

BRYANT. Don't be salty. He said he dreams about killing Uncle Cecil. That's crazy.

JAMES. He's crazy.

BRYANT. Is it ironic or a coincidence that you saved Bubba with the knife Uncle C gave you? I think I always get those mixed up.

(A breath.)

James!

JAMES. It's an ironic coincidence.

BRYANT. Oh. Damn I'm not tired.

JAMES. Read a book.

BRYANT. Didn't bring one.

JAMES. Read one of their books.

BRYANT. All they got is, mystery, romance novels and like architecture textbooks books.

JAMES. B.

BRYANT. I'm going to go look for Emory. I'm taking a walk. You coming?

JAMES. No. Go.

> (**BRYANT** *exits. He opens the door slowly and slips out so as not to make too much noise.*)
>
> (*He yells through the screen door:*)

BRYANT. I'LL BE BACK YO!

> (**JAMES** *spasms, startled.* **CHERYL** *gets up.* **CECIL** *mumbles inaudible words.* **CHERYL** *leans in close to better hear him.*)

CHERYL. Because I can't. No. Stop asking me!

> (*She quickly moves out of the back room and walks to the front.*)

James?

JAMES. What?!

CHERYL. Boy!

JAMES. Sorry. Sorry.

CHERYL. Where's your brother and Bubba?

JAMES. Went for a walk.

CHERYL. This early in the morning?

JAMES. Apparently.

CHERYL. I'm going to make coffee. Want some?

JAMES. No.

(A minute.)

CHERYL. I am really happy you and your brother decided to visit.

JAMES. Mm.

CHERYL. Don't know how much longer Cecil got and Emory...he's been a lot to deal with lately, even more than when he was younger. I just can't gauge him, sometimes he's him and sometimes he's not. You guys have changed too. Well no, not Bryant he's exactly the same. You're.

Different.

Are you sad?

I know you're not asleep.

(JAMES fake snores.)

Don't be an asshole.

JAMES. Aunt Cheryl, language.

CHERYL. Child spare me. It's too early.

(JAMES chuckles. A moment.)

Tell me a story like you would when you were younger. You always told the best stories, and what would you say? Before you'd start you'd say –

CHERYL.	**JAMES.**
Drama time.	Drama time.

CHERYL. Not that there's not enough drama going on right now but I just need //...

JAMES. Do you remember that one Easter we stayed with you.

CHERYL. Yes. You got that olive-colored suit you had all dirty and full of holes, your mother bitches about that to this day.

JAMES. Bitches?

CHERYL. I haven't had my coffee.

Tell your story.

> *(A breath. A light change.* **JAMES** *is now twelve years old.)*

JAMES. You, Bubba and Bryant were at church helping clean up after Easter brunch. I asked you if I could come back to the house because...

Aunt Cheryl I have a stomachache can I go back to the house please?

"Okay baby, take your suit off as soon as you get home, before you lay down or anything else, you hear?"

I got you.

"Excuse me?"

Yes, ma'am...

But I didn't really have a stomachache I wanted to see Kerry-Anne Miller.

CHERYL. Kerry-Anne Miller? Kerry-Anne Miller, had the lazy eye?

JAMES. She had a dope body.

CHERYL. The white girl that lives a few houses down? Dope? Mm.

That eye made her look like she smoked dope.

JAMES. Can I finish my story please?

CHERYL. Mm.

JAMES. So I went to her house, in my suit because I knew I looked good.

Kerry-Anne! Kerry-Anne! Come outside real quick.

> (**MAX** and **SAM** *[played by* **BRYANT** *and* **EMORY***] enter from the back. They speak with overly affected Southern accents.*)

MAX. Well would ya lookie her'. Ain't you one of dem New York City twins that don't look a nothin' alike.

CHERYL. Who was talking like that?

JAMES. Shh.

SAM. Whatcha doin' round here boy.

JAMES. I came to holla at Kerry-Anne real quick.

MAX. You "came to holla at Kerry-Anne real quick."

SAM. Oh no boy you didn't.

> (*He grabs* **JAMES**, *pinning his arms behind him.* **MAX** *punches* **JAMES** *three times in the gut.* **JAMES** *falls to the ground, gasping for air.* **SAM** *and* **MAX** *laugh at him.*)

JAMES. They knocked the wind out of me and I never felt that before. I thought I was dying so I started to cry. I cried and gasped all the way back here and Uncle Cecil was on the porch working on the screen door.

> (**CECIL** *emerges from the back room. His accent is just as overly Southern affected.*)

CECIL. What the hell wrong with your citified self now.

JAMES. They they they they they punched me.

CECIL. Well did you punch 'em back?

JAMES. I I I I I I...

CECIL. Who is "they"?

JAMES. Ker, Ker, Kerry...bro, bro, bro...

CECIL. You let some white boys whoop on you?

Take your tail back up that road and don't you come back unless you won you that fight.

JAMES. So I turned around and went to fight, because I was way more afraid of Uncle Cecil.

SAM. You back for more boy?

MAX. Some just don' kno' when ta get when tha gettin's good.

> (**MAX** *and* **SAM** *jump on* **JAMES.** *They scuffle and tussle, and* **JAMES** *puts up a good effort, but he's always on the losing end. They eventually pin him down and pull down his pants and underwear.)*

SAM. Now walk back home with your trousers round your ankles boy.

MAX. And if you try to pull'm up we gon' whoop ya good agin.

CECIL. Boy what in the hell?

> *(He grabs a belt and starts whipping* **JAMES** *with it.)*

Must be out your gourd walkin' round here with your pants down. Good Christian folks live round here!

> (**CECIL, SAM,** *and* **MAX** *exit through the back.* **CECIL** *returns to his bed.* **CHERYL** *is laughing hysterically. A light change.)*

CHERYL. I'm sorry baby. I don't mean to laugh so hard. It's just the way you tell it.

JAMES. Worst part is, when you got back and saw my suit you licked me a few times with the extension cord.

CHERYL. Ooh. I did not.

JAMES. Yes you did. Tore the back of my legs up.

CHERYL. I'm sorry. I'm so sorry.

JAMES. Yeah I can tell.

CHERYL. Come here.

JAMES. You gonna beat me?

CHERYL. No really come here.

*(She hugs **JAMES**.)*

Your uncle and I grew up in harsher times, it was how we were raised.

JAMES. Whatever. It is what it is. And so concludes "drama time."

*(**BRYANT** screams offstage. The screen door cries out, and **BRYANT** stumbles in with **EMORY** close behind. The screen door slams.)*

EMORY. I'm sorry I'm sorry I'm sorry. I didn't mean to…

*(**BRYANT** has James' knife stuck deep in his shoulder where only the handle is visible.)*

CHERYL. Oh my Jesus, what happened?

EMORY. He he he, I, I…

JAMES. You stabbed my brother?!

BRYANT. It's not his fault. He didn't mean to…

(He woozily drops to one knee.)

JAMES. You stabbed my brother?! You piece of shit!

CHERYL. Stop it! Emory go grab my purse from out the room. Now!

JAMES. Hang in there B. Don't die please don't die.

CHERYL. He's not going to die. James listen I need you to stay here with Cecil while I take your brother to the hospital. JAMES!! Focus now. He's going to be fine. Emory you're coming with us.

> (**EMORY** *holds open the screen door.* **CHERYL** *guides* **BRYANT** *out the door.* **EMORY** *follows. The screen door slams.* **JAMES** *stands motionless.* **CECIL** *moans in pain.* **JAMES** *walks to the back room.)*

JAMES. Uncle Cecil.

Please don't die. We need you.

CECIL. James. James.

IV.

(A light change. A minute. **BRYANT** *is asleep on the air mattress.* **JAMES** *sits on the floor next to him.* **CHERYL** *kneels praying on the floor of the middle room.* **CECIL** *moans in pain.* **EMORY** *stands in a shirt and boxer briefs. He watches over* **CECIL** *in the back room.* **CECIL** *mumbles inaudible words.* **EMORY** *leans close to hear him.)*

EMORY. Okay Daddy.

(He moves from the back room to the front. He peeks his head into the middle room.)

Ma, I'm getting Dad some water. I think he wants water.

*(**CHERYL** does not acknowledge. A moment. **EMORY** moves to the front room and walks to the fridge. He opens it, pulls out the water container, and pours a glass.)*

JAMES. I should've let you die. I should've let you die. I should've let you die.

EMORY. It was an accident. He snuck up behind me. I got scared.

JAMES. I should've let you die.

(A breath. **EMORY** *moves to the back room.)*

Hang yourself again. Please. So I can watch you swing.

*(**CHERYL** calls to **EMORY** as he moves past her room.)*

CHERYL. Bubba.

EMORY. Yes?

CHERYL. Come here son.

>   (**EMORY** *comes into the room.* **CHERYL** *gets up, walks to* **EMORY**, *takes the glass, and drinks down the water.*)

EMORY. Mom that was for...

CHERYL. Come lie down with me, Bubba.

EMORY. Mom, Daddy...

CHERYL. He doesn't want water, Bubba. He wants to pass on.

EMORY. But...

CHERYL. He's not saying "water," he's saying "why?"

>   (*A moment.*)

He wants to die. He doesn't want to be in pain anymore and before he left the hospital he asked me to give him his gun. I told him no. He's been asking "why not" since. Come lie down. You are your father's son.

I'm sorry.

EMORY. It's okay Mom. It's okay. I'm sorry I'm not a good son. I'll take care of you.

CHERYL. Oh god. Bubba. I don't trust you. I'm sorry. I know that's a horrible thing for a mother to say. God forgive me, but I don't.

EMORY. I didn't mean to stab Bry. It was an accident!

CHERYL. I'm not talking about that. Your father is going to be gone very soon now. Didn't want the surgery or the radiation. Refused it all. Nothing. Just came home to die. His pride trumps twenty years.

Just try; that's all. Am I really asking for too much? Am I? Am I?

And you.

I'm going to be alone.

Both of the men I love most in this world are leaving me. Neither of them are willing to fight. Fight for me. You're both just quitting. Quitting and leaving me alone. You don't think there have been times I've wanted to quit? Just lay it all down? But no I don't have that luxury, never had that luxury.

So I'm mourning now. There are going to be funeral arrangements that have to be made and hospital bills and life and life will go on and I can't be mourning. I won't have the time. So I'm doing it now. I wish I could trust that you'll be there for me but I don't. I don't.

Come lie down next to me.

> (**CHERYL** *and* **EMORY** *lie together.* **JAMES** *lies next to* **BRYANT** *on the air mattress.* **CECIL** *lies alone.)*

V.

(A moment. A light change. **BRYANT** *stands at the fridge with the door open. His arm wrapped up and in a sling.* **JAMES** *is carrying their bags out to the car.* **EMORY** *stands next to* **BRYANT**. **CHERYL** *deflates the air mattress.)*

CHERYL. What did I tell you about leaving that fridge door open?

BRYANT. I'm a crippled man Aunt Cheryl, a brother gotta do things slow like.

CHERYL. Well I'm about to kick you out fast like.

BRYANT. Aww man, where's the love? Where is the love?

EMORY. Bry, I'm sorry man.

BRYANT. Stop apologizing cuzzo. It's all good.

JAMES. Let's go, we're going to miss our flight.

BRYANT. Chill. Hey, Em seriously no worries bro. I jerk off with my left hand anyway.

*(***EMORY*** chuckles.)*

Oh shit. I got you. Damn man I coulda been making masturbation jokes from the jump. Now I know.

*(***EMORY*** and ***BRYANT*** hug.)*

Love you man. Be here next time I come back.

EMORY. Okay.

BRYANT. Aunt Cheryl! We out! Tell your son to put some pants on; it's weird.

CHERYL. I can't ever send you boys home in one piece.

BRYANT. That's what makes this hot-ass, racist-ass town exciting. You never know who's gonna get ya.

(CHERYL and BRYANT hug and kiss. JAMES opens the door and holds it open for BRYANT.)

JAMES. Come on man.

CHERYL. Did you say goodbye to your uncle?

BRYANT. Yep.

(He walks out. JAMES steps in the doorway to give CHERYL a kiss.)

JAMES. Bye. Be careful. I'm not coming back.

CHERYL. You two take care of each other.

Have a good year at school.

(JAMES exits. The screen door cries out and slams. The sound of a vehicle's engine and tires on a gravel road. EMORY walks to the back room. CHERYL continues deflating the air mattress. EMORY watches his father. CHERYL walks to the fridge, opens it, takes out the pitcher of iced tea, and drinks directly from the pitcher. EMORY gets closer to his father and discovers CECIL is dead. EMORY drops to his knees.)

(CHERYL moves to the middle room. She opens the dresser, sees and pulls out the noose. EMORY kneels at his father's bedside.)

PART II

VI.

(Packed and sealed cardboard boxes fill the back room. Only the bed and the basin remain. The other rooms are stark and stripped to a bare minimum. No art, figurines or family photos. The linen on the bed in the middle room is plain and reminiscent of what one would see in a hospital. **EMORY** *lies on top of the sheets in the fetal position. He is fully dressed, wearing an all-black suit. He lowly mumbles to himself. The ghosts of the past can be seen in the two-toned outlines on the walls and floor left by removed mirrors, pictures, chairs, and furniture. Only the kitchen area remains fully intact and untouched. In the front room there are two long folding tables touching end to end, shaping an L. On the tables, an assortment of food is spread out: collard greens, mac and cheese, yams, sweet potatoes, chicken [fried and baked], ribs, baked ziti, fish, cornbread... etc. All of the food is close to or totally gone, except for an untouched container full of potato salad. A few metal folding chairs lean against the wall. Behind the translucent wall is the figure of* **UNCLE CECIL** *sitting in a rocking chair. Periodically the figure rocks in the chair.)*

(CHERYL, BRYANT, LYNN, *and* JAMES *enter.* CHERYL, LYNN, *and* JAMES *wear all-black funeral attire.* BRYANT's *suit is a dark navy and his arm is in a sling.* JAMES *does not enter all the way; he stands at the doorway.*)

BRYANT. You sure you don't want help cleaning up?

LYNN. Says the cripple.

BRYANT. All I need is one arm. This arm won't fail me!

(He kisses his bicep and does a bodybuilder pose.)

LYNN. You got one brain and that fails you all the time.

BRYANT. Ma, you ain't right.

CHERYL. I'll be fine. Y'all go ahead back to the motel. It's been a long day.

BRYANT. Can I take some of this leftover food to the telly with us for a midnight...?

CHERYL. Of course baby. Help yourself.

(BRYANT gets aluminum foil from a kitchen drawer and begins to build to-go plates.)

LYNN. Why didn't anyone touch my potato salad?

(A moment.)

BRYANT. Everyone must've been full by the time they got to it?

LYNN. Oh well, their loss. More for us.

JAMES. Your potato salad tastes like shit.

CHERYL.	BRYANT.
James?!	Bro?!

LYNN. You ain't said nothin' all day and that's the first words you speak? And why you standing at the door? Whatchu a vampire or some shit?

JAMES. Tired of this family pretending all the damn time.

LYNN. Whatchu say boy?!

CHERYL. Lynn let him be.

LYNN. Lucky your father couldn't come down with us, all that lip would come up missing.

(EMORY enters the front room.)

BRYANT. Bubs you want me to leave you some of this chicken? Speak now.

(JAMES exits.)

LYNN. He must've lost his mind.

CHERYL. He's sad. Let him be.

LYNN. Talking about my potato salad. My salad is damn good.

(A moment.)

Bubba my potato salad is good right?

EMORY. No ma'am. Not really.

LYNN. Aw whatta you know. You're crazy.

CHERYL. Lynn.

LYNN. I'm teasing.

CHERYL. Y'all sure you don't want to just stay here instead of paying for that //...

LYNN. No. We're fine.

Why don't you just pack the whole table in the car?!

(**BRYANT** *has made and stacked multiple plates of food and attempts to carry and balance them with his one hand.*)

CHERYL. Bubba help your cousin bring his food to the car.

EMORY. Yes ma'am.

BRYANT. I'm good. If next week's surgery doesn't work to repair my nerves I'm going to have to learn how to rock like this anyway.

LYNN. While you're under they need to open up your head see what nerves are damaged in there.

(**EMORY** *takes a couple of plates from* **BRYANT**'s *stack.*)

BRYANT. You ain't right.

LYNN. YOU ain't right.

BRYANT. See you tomorrow Aunt Cheryl. Yo what happened to the screen door?

CHERYL. Oh I fixed it.

BRYANT. Work it out Mrs. HGTV.

LYNN. Screen doors are useless if they're held open.

BRYANT. Bye, love you.

CHERYL. Okay baby. Love you too.

(**BRYANT** *exits with* **EMORY** *close behind. Outside the sound of a car-door slam and the faint sound of a dog barking. A minute.*)

(**EMORY** *enters.*)

LYNN. Hey! You know I should snap your scrawny neck right? You know that right?

CHERYL. Lynn.

LYNN. Hm? You know that right? Huh?

EMORY. Yes ma'am.

LYNN. You hear me boy?

EMORY. Yes ma'am.

(A moment.)

LYNN. You're the man of the house now. You can't be runnin' around here acting crazy no more. Yeah?

EMORY. Uh-huh.

LYNN. All right now that's my boy. Here take this.

*(She hands **EMORY** a pill bottle.)*

It's Abilify. I got Tony to write a prescription. Let's see if these get your head screwed on right.

CHERYL. Bubba take those four chairs back over to the Millers' for me please.

*(**EMORY** collects the chairs. **LYNN** holds the door open for him. **EMORY** exits. **LYNN** watches him for a moment.)*

Lynn I need you not to be You these next couple of days. You have to be more sensitive to…

LYNN. What's going on with you?

CHERYL. What?

LYNN. The dismantling of the house, you barely looking at or speaking to Emory, you hardly spoke to anyone after the funeral.

CHERYL. Funeral. Key word. My husband.

My husband is dead. Maybe that's what's going on with me.

LYNN. I know you. This isn't you. Grief or no grief.

CHERYL. Lynn for once in our lives spare me your pseudo-psycho babble.

LYNN. Oh no you did… It wasn't pseudo when I put my job at CVS in danger and mail you them pills for little Emory's butt.

CHERYL. What does that have to do with… Could we not do this today. Please. Have some respect for something or someone for once.

LYNN. Here we go. See I knew there was something bubbling under there…

CHERYL There ain't nothing bubbling under nowhere. It's all bubbled out.

LYNN. You not forgiving me is keeping you trapped. All these years…

CHERYL. It's not about you! You selfish bitch. Shut up. Just shut your mouth.

(A minute.)

(LYNN bursts into laughter.)

LYNN. Wow. I haven't heard you cuss at me like that since, it's been a long time. How'd it feel? Felt good huh?

CHERYL. No.

Lynn.

I.

LYNN. We'll be back tomorrow. Tomorrow.

Too much today. You're right I'm not being sensitive. Okay? Tomorrow.

Make sure you put my potato salad in the fridge, we'll have some tomorrow.

*(She moves as if she wants to hug **CHERYL**, decides against it, and exits. Outside sound*

of a car-door slam and tires on a gravel road.
CHERYL *surveys the room, picks up the potato salad from the table. Puts it back down where it was, walks to the middle room, and lies down on the bed. She waits and listens, unsure what exactly she's listening for. She falls asleep.)*

VII.

(The morning. **CHERYL** *sleeps in the bed, still wearing her funeral clothes.* **LYNN, JAMES,** *and* **BRYANT** *clean the front room, washing and putting away the dishes.* **BRYANT** *breaks down the folding tables.* **JAMES** *starts to reluctantly sweep the floor.* **LYNN** *periodically shoots looks of disgust toward* **JAMES. EMORY,** *also still in his funeral clothes, sits on the floor in the back room among all the boxes.)*

LYNN. If you swept up the right way you'd be done quicker.

Can't believe she forgot to put my potato salad in the fridge. It tastes best when it's cold.

(A minute.)

Was she like this when you two were here?

BRYANT. Like what?

> *(He walks to the fridge, pulls out a pill container, opens it, and taps a pill into his mouth. Then he pulls the pitcher of iced tea out and takes a swig.)*

LYNN. Take it easy with those.

Like, Not Cheryl.

BRYANT. No she seemed like herself. Right J?

LYNN. Your brother is talking to you. What is with you and this mute act? Huh? HUH?

JAMES. Nothing.

LYNN. You know there are five stages of grief and silently bitchy isn't one of them.

> *(***BRYANT** *chuckles.* **JAMES** *looks as if he wants to speak, but instead turns to walk out the front*

door; still holding the broom, he accidentally pokes a hole in the screen. **CHERYL** *wakes.*)

BRYANT. Oh! Score!

LYNN. Nice.

JAMES. Shit.

LYNN. Your aunt is trying to sell this house you know? Holes in shit; depreciates value.

(**CHERYL** *enters the room.*)

CHERYL. Oh lord. What happened?

(**BRYANT** *grabs his crotch and starts thrusting toward* **JAMES'** *direction.*)

BRYANT. You've been hit by – you've been struck by – Whewww!

(*He does a spin move and goes up on his toes.*)

JAMES. I didn't mean to...

(*He looks as if he's going to cry.* **BRYANT** *notices.*)

BRYANT. Jay?

(**JAMES** *quickly exits.*)

LYNN. James Cecil Walker come back here! James. James.

(*She exits. Outside, the faint sound of a dog barking.*)

BRYANT. That was dramatic.

CHERYL. I knew Cecil's death was going to be hard on him but this is...

BRYANT. It's hard on all of us Aunt Cheryl.

CHERYL. Yes. Yes it is.

*(**EMORY** walks into the front room.)*

BRYANT. Bubbalious what up cuz?

EMORY. Hey.

(He exits.)

BRYANT. What tha? Damn talk about "drama time."

*(**CHERYL** sighs.)*

Well Aunt Cheryl looks like we're the only ones not in a Tyler Perry film.

(He examines the hole in the screen door.)

So when are you selling?

CHERYL. As soon as someone's buying.

BRYANT. Where you gonna go?

CHERYL. Back to Michigan.

BRYANT. The D?

CHERYL. Lansing most likely.

BRYANT. You and Em should come to New York.

CHERYL. You going to give me some "come to New York" money?

BRYANT. Um.

CHERYL. Uh-huh. New York City is more your mother's scene anyway.

BRYANT. Long Island can't really be considered the New York scene. But I feel you on the money tip. I did research for a microeconomics class last semester; yo, taxes on Long Island are stupid. Stupid.

CHERYL. How's your arm?

BRYANT. Hurts. It's crazy if I take the sling off my arm will just fall. I can move my fingers but my elbow and shoulder is a wrap. Doctor said it's a severe brachial plexus injury. The Vicodin helps with the pain a little but I guess my wound is healing so there's this itch on like the inside that's driving me cray.

CHERYL. Be careful with that Vicodin.

BRYANT. I know. I know. Mom tells me every other second.

CHERYL. How's she been doing?

BRYANT. Fine. More importantly how are you? You're still rocking your clothes from yesterday.

CHERYL. Yeah. I passed out. I was just so exhausted. I'm going to go shower now. Thank you for cleaning up out here.

BRYANT. No doubt.

Aunt Cheryl.

You been keeping an eye on Bubba?

CHERYL. He's going to do what he's going to do.

BRYANT. But.

CHERYL. He's going to do what he's going to do.

(She moves to the middle room and takes out clothes to change into. Outside, the sound of a car door, tires on a gravel road, and the faint sound of a dog barking.)

BRYANT. Damn.

*(**JAMES** enters.)*

The prodigal son return-eth.

(A moment.)

(The barking stops.)

BRYANT. Where's Mom?

JAMES. Cigarette run.

BRYANT. What's up bro?

> *(A moment.)*

Jay?

JAMES. Nothing.

BRYANT. Yo, you've been weird since before Uncle C passed. Since Em accidently stabbed me.

JAMES. "Accidently." I can't believe we're related to that kid.

BRYANT. It was an accident man! Just like you just jousted the hell outta the screen door.

> *(A moment.)*

JAMES. You remember when Cecil would tell us about dying, dying for a reason?

BRYANT. "If you can have a say in it, die for a cause."

JAMES. Yeah.

BRYANT. What's up J?

JAMES. Emory is going to off himself eventually right? So //...

BRYANT. You don't know that.

JAMES. So why don't we help him and stage it as something that can bring about change.

> *(A minute. **CHERYL** leaves the bedroom for the bathroom.)*

BRYANT. You been smokin' that dust?

JAMES. Like stage an Emmett Till copy-cat murder that sheds light on the racism that still exists.

BRYANT. Aren't you supposed to be the smart twin?

JAMES. B, I'm serious!

BRYANT. Nigga I see that! Look man I don't know what's up with you, but we ain't helping our baby cousin kill himself.

JAMES. With all the shit in the news we could spark // –

BRYANT. NO! End of discussion. There's so much wrong with… Yo, let's say for argument's sake murder was an okay thing. My dude, we desensitized to Black death so ain't no change gonna come. "Stage a copy-cat Emmett Till"… You are officially on some shit.

JAMES. He stabbed you. He dreams about killing Aunt Cheryl!

BRYANT. It was an…

 (**EMORY** *enters. His hands are bloody.*)

What the…

 (**JAMES** *springs to the screen door and looks outside.*)

JAMES. Ma! MOM!

What did you do!

EMORY. You know the Robinsons' dog the one that chased you way back when? He barked at me.

 (*A breath.*)

BRYANT. So you?

JAMES. Crazy little…

EMORY. He barked at me and it was like he was threatening me. And you. And you and our family. He was barking threats at our family. And Daddy always said he always said if a man threatens your family you take him out first. Protect your family at all costs, never give no one or nothing the opportunity to make good on their threats.

BRYANT. It was a dog.

EMORY. It only barked at us only ever seen it bark at us.

JAMES. This nigger here.

BRYANT. You killed your neighbors' dog. Bubba that's a problem. For real for real.

JAMES. Fucking "accident."

BRYANT. James not the time bro.

JAMES. Why are you always defending him?

BRYANT. What?

JAMES. I'm your brother. Me!

EMORY. Bark. Bark bark bark bark. Bark...

BRYANT. Are y'all serious? Am I being punked right now?

JAMES. Look at him! He's gone!

EMORY. James. James would never save you. If he got loose James would let you get ate.

JAMES. Shut up! You stabbed my brother, killed some damn dog and probably Uncle Cecil.

BRYANT. Whoa hey Jay, easy. Be easy bro.

EMORY. He would never save you Bry, you know that.

(Loudly whispers.) He's a pussy.

JAMES. Bitch!

EMORY. Bark bark bark bark bark.

BRYANT. Y'all are trippin'. Chill!

(Outside, the sound of tires on gravel and a door slam. **LYNN** *enters.)*

LYNN. I got us all some ice pops and some tampons for James. Way he's acting I figure he must be...

(She sees the blood on **EMORY**.*)*

Shit! Are you okay! What happened?!

(She checks **EMORY**'s *body for wounds.)*

CHERYL! Where's your mother? CHERYL!

*(**CHERYL** moves into the front room, sees that **EMORY** is bloody but doesn't move.)*

CHERYL. What happened?

BRYANT. Bubba killed the neighbors' dog.

LYNN. What?

CHERYL. So you're all right?

EMORY. Yes ma'am.

LYNN. Hold on. You killed a dog? The neighbors' dog?

CHERYL. Take off those clothes and go get cleaned up.

LYNN. What?

EMORY. Yes ma'am.

(He moves to the back room. Takes off his clothes, retrieves the bucket, gets into the basin tub, and proceeds to clean himself.)

LYNN. You're not going to ask him what happened?

CHERYL. Bryant already said, he killed the neighbors' dog. Is that right Bry?

BRYANT. Um. Yeah. Yeah that's what he said.

LYNN. Cheryl?

CHERYL. What do you want me to do Lynn? Walk over to the Robinsons', it's the Robinsons' dog isn't it?

JAMES. Yeah.

CHERYL. I'm going to walk over there. Tell them that my son just murdered their dog. They'll call the police. Probably threaten to sue me. The police will come, if they don't kill him they'll most likely take Bubba down to the station. I won't be able to bail him out till Monday morning, meanwhile I have a meeting with the MetLife agent about Cecil's life insurance Monday, and a meeting with my real estate agent about a potential buyer for the house. Oh and I have to fix my screen door.

Lynn you get to fly out with the boys whenever the hell you're leaving and I me I have to deal with all the fallout. Me. Not you. Me.

(A moment.)

LYNN. Cheryl. I'm. Hey let's just.

CHERYL. Excuse me I have to go talk to the Robinsons. Do me a favor and make sure my son is dressed by the time the police come.

(She exits.)

LYNN. Okay. What just happened here?

JAMES. You know.

(A moment.)

BRYANT. Well I don't! Is Bubba's crazy contagious or something?

JAMES. Or something.

VIII.

(A light change. **EMORY** *sits in the tub. He cleans the blood off, then dresses without drying off. Lights shift as if in "drama time."* **EMORY**'s *speech cadence becomes similar to Cecil's.)*

EMORY. Something wrong with the shower? I think you've outgrown that basin by about fifteen years now. You protesting towels? At least you're clean right? Your granddad wasn't much of a talker. Only time I remember him stringing more than two sentences together was when he was angry and cussing us out. Did I ever tell you about the time I decided to be silent to see how long it would take until Dad would notice I wasn't talking? Went a whole year and then one night he looks up from his glass of bourbon and says, "You're awfully quiet tonight Cecil."

When you become a parent you try not to be... I don't know you Emory. You walk around this house and I don't understand how you think and it's my fault. I know it's my fault and I'm sorry. I'm sorry and now I don't have the time. Whatever you do don't ever live with regret, you hear me? Don't you ever live with regret.

(He lets out a sound drenched in pain and frustration. A high-pitched tone swells; noises fill the room. He paces for a second, then goes to a box on the floor in the corner. He opens it and pulls out three prescription bottles. He examines the bottles for a moment, then opens them and carefully empties their contents on the floor. He sits in front of the pile of pills on the floor and admires it. He stands up and walks to the front room. He goes to the fridge and pulls out the pitcher

of iced tea and walks to the back room with the pitcher. He sits back in front of his pile of pills. Picks one out of the pile, puts it into his mouth, takes a swig from the pitcher, and swallows. Waits a minute, then repeats: pill, mouth, swig, swallow. Waits a minute. Pill. Mouth. Swig. Swallow.)

(LYNN, JAMES, and BRYANT enter through the front door.)

LYNN. Bubba!

Emory!

EMORY. Yes ma'am!

(Pill. Mouth. Swig. Swallow.)

LYNN. Nothing just seeing where you are!

Cheryl has her hands full boys I think we're going to stay an extra day or two.

BRYANT. Aight.

JAMES. Great.

LYNN. What is your problem? Seriously?

JAMES. I don't want to be here. That's all. It's hot, Emory's crazy. I don't want to be here.

LYNN. It's always hot. Always been hot and Bubba's always been some form of crazy.

JAMES. And when have I ever expressed liking it here? You made us go so we came.

BRYANT. Don't be we-ing. I always looked forward to seeing the fam. And you know what man so did you at one point. You be bullshittin'.

LYNN. You do be bullshittin'.

JAMES. (Not as much as you.)

BRYANT. Whoa.

LYNN. Boy I will smack the taste out of you mouth. Emory's crazy must be contagious.

(Pill. Mouth. Swig. Swallow.)

BRYANT. Must be this heat! Oh but I know the remedy.

LYNN. Talk to me like that again. Come out your face one more time.

*(**BRYANT** goes to the fridge. Pulls his Vicodin out of his pocket.)*

BRYANT. Aw man where the iced tea at?

(He places the Vicodin on the counter.)

LYNN. Have an ice pop.

BRYANT. Word. Forgot about those.

LYNN. So James what is your problem?

JAMES. Nothing.

*(**BRYANT** pulls out an ice pop from the freezer.)*

BRYANT. I love these but there's no way to eat them and not look gay. I mean you could just bite 'em but the cold jacks up my teeth.

LYNN. Bryant. Enough.

James what is with this sudden disrespectful attitude?

BRYANT. Sudden?

(Pill. Mouth. Swig. Swallow.)

LYNN. Bryant.

*(She shoots **BRYANT** a "if I have to tell you again" motherly look.)*

BRYANT. Sorry.

LYNN. I wish your father was here.

>(**JAMES** *laughs heartily.* **CHERYL** *enters.*)

CHERYL. They decided not to press charges.

BRYANT. Whaaat?! Now that's crazy.

CHERYL. What's so funny?

>(*Pill. Mouth. Swig. Swallow.*)

LYNN. That's what I'd like to know?

JAMES. Everything. Everything is just funny.

LYNN. Everything?

BRYANT. How'd you pull off getting them not to press charges?

CHERYL. They know we've been going through tough times. Said they didn't want to add to the misery. No point.

>(*Pill. Mouth. Swig. Swallow.*)

BRYANT. Wow. Matrix bullet dodge.

JAMES. Fucking Bullshit. Emory needs to be locked the fuck up or dead!

CHERYL. James?

>(**LYNN** *slaps* **JAMES.**)

>(*Pill. Mouth. Swig. Swallow.*)

Lynn!

LYNN. I've had enough of you acting like some spoiled little white bitch. Your grief pass is expired. Done. Now apologize to your aunt for being disrespectful.

>(*A moment.*)

JAMES. Did you ever apologize to her?

LYNN. Excuse me?

JAMES. For being disrespectful, did you ever apologize?

> *(Pill. Mouth. Pill. Mouth. Pill. Mouth. Swig. Swallow.)*
>
> *(A moment.)*

Probably huh? Probably did a bunch of apologizing. Well I'm sorry Aunt Cheryl. I'm sorry for using profanity in your house. I'm sorry I refuse to act like there's nothing wrong with Emory like he's not psycho no matter how much Xanax or Lithium or whatever we pump into him.

> *(Pill. Mouth. Swig. Swallow.)*

LYNN. Hey!

JAMES. I'm sorry I'm not the same fun "Drama Time" kid you remember. I'm sorry I came back here when I didn't want to I'm sorry... I'm sorry Emory stabbed Bry. I'm sorry Emory stabbed Bry.

CHERYL. Why are you sorry about // –

JAMES. You guys left me. Left me with –

Cecil. Left me alone and I was scared that Emory might have...that Bry could've died and I went to the back room to check on.

I thought what if what if Bryant dies and at the same time Cecil dies like they're connected somehow so I thought by watching him I thought I'd know what was happening with Bry from watching. Most irrational thought but...

CHERYL. Take your time baby. What are you saying?

(Pill. Mouth. Pill. Mouth. Pill. Mouth. Swig. Swallow.)

JAMES. He was awake and looking at me and I was scared. I was scared. The way he looked at me I knew he wanted to say something. Tell me something I didn't want to know.

LYNN. Oh my god.

CHERYL. Oh Cecil.

BRYANT. What? What I miss? What? What?!

LYNN. Dammit Cecil!

BRYANT. Could someone please tell me what's going on please? Jay? Mom? Aunt Cheryl? Hello? Out of the loop dot com over here.

JAMES. Bro every time I tried to tell you I punked out.

BRYANT. That's 'cause you're a punk.

My dude. What?

(A moment.)

LYNN. Cecil's your father.

(Pill. Mouth. Swig. Swallow.)

(A minute.)

BRYANT. Um. Um. Okay. Yeah. Yep. Sure. Why not? Right? Why not? So dude back in New York I've been calling Dad is? And wait? So Uncle C and Mom?

LYNN. It's complicated Bry.

BRYANT. Really? Really? Complicated? Yeah that's ahh, that's ahh a bit of an understatement. Does Emory know?

JAMES. Who cares?

LYNN. Nobody knew.

BRYANT. Right. Right. Okay. So at the funeral I cried Uncle tears when I should've been shedding Daddy tears. Right.

CHERYL. Bry.

BRYANT. No. no. no. no. no. no. Nope. My mom. James. Cecil. I know they could be on that secretive tip with me but you Aunt Cheryl? I helped you change this dude's diaper at no point did you think maybe I should know the penis I was looking at was the one that gave me life?

LYNN. Enough.

BRYANT. No I don't think so. I need more. We need more. A whole lot more.

JAMES. Tons.

>   *(Pill. Pill. Pill. Pill. Pill. Pill. Pill. Pill. Mouth. Swig. Swallow.)*

CHERYL. That's fair.

It'll be a relief actually.

BRYANT. Emory should be here for this.

LYNN. No Bryant.

CHERYL. Yes Lynn. He's right.

>   (**BRYANT** *moves to the back room.* **EMORY** *has taken all the pills.*)

BRYANT. Hey you need to come to the front.

EMORY. Cops here to take me?

BRYANT. Oh no. You dodged that bullet my dude. This is going to be way more traumatic. Hope you took your pills.

(**EMORY** *gets up.*)

BRYANT. Oh so you stole the iced tea.

EMORY. Sorry.

BRYANT. Look you're about to hear some cray shit in a second. Don't flip out.

EMORY. I'm fine.

(**BRYANT** *and* **EMORY** *walk back to the front room.*)

BRYANT. Enlighten us.

LYNN. How are you feeling Bubba?

BRYANT. Stop stalling.

EMORY. I'm fine Auntie Lynn.

JAMES. Great. So now how is it we're brothers and not cousins?

EMORY. Wha?

BRYANT. Shh. We're about to find out.

LYNN. You want me to tell it or do you?

CHERYL. I'd actually love to hear your side of it actually.

LYNN. Okay. Well. Your aunt was engaged to Cecil and um this was this was –

JAMES. About nineteen years ago.

LYNN. Yes. Well. Um.

(A minute.)

Emory your father has always loved your mother, okay. You need to know that.

JAMES. Stop catering to him!

LYNN. You yelling at me will not happen again James.

CHERYL. James please.

LYNN. My patience and my guilt are not connected in any way.

BRYANT. Mom.

(**EMORY** *nods as if fighting sleep.*)

LYNN. Em are you okay?

EMORY. I'm fine.

(*He collapses to the floor.*)

LYNN. Emory!

BRYANT. Bub? Bub? Em?

JAMES. I hope this is it.

CHERYL. I'll call the ambulance.

LYNN. Wake up. Wake up honey. You're going to be all right. You're going to be all right. Emory we're here we're right here you're going to be okay.

(**BRYANT** *walks out the front door.*)

Bry! Bry! Shit. Hold on Emory. Hold on baby. Help is coming. Help is coming.

IX.

(Evening. **BRYANT** *lies on the floor of the front room.)*

BRYANT.
NOBODY KNOWS THE TROUBLE I SEEN.
NOOOOBODY KNOWS MY SORROW.
NOOOOBODY KNOWS THE TROUBLE I SEEEEEEEN.

(Outside, the sound of tires on the gravel road and a car-door slam. **CHERYL** *enters.)*

CHERYL. I really should fix that screen so we don't get ate up.

BRYANT. I think I lost a quart of blood already.

CHERYL. Not mad at me anymore?

BRYANT. No. It's moved to Mom.

CHERYL. Shouldn't be mad at her either.

BRYANT. Where they at?

CHERYL. At the hospital with Emory, keeping him overnight for observation.

BRYANT. You left?

CHERYL. Had my fill of the hospital.

BRYANT. Oh. Yeah.

James stayed?

CHERYL. Your mother made him.

BRYANT. Of course.

CHERYL. Mind if I join you?

BRYANT. Nah.

CHERYL. Nah?

BRYANT. No I don't mind.

(**CHERYL** *lies on the floor.*)

CHERYL. God I really need to mop.

BRYANT. I counted like a hundred dust bunnies.

CHERYL. Oh you did not.

(A tension-relief laugh.)

(A moment.)

BRYANT. So my father huh?

CHERYL. Uh-huh.

BRYANT. This story's ratchet, isn't it?

CHERYL. I don't know what that means but it sounds like the appropriate word.

(A moment.)

"Drama time."

(A light change. **CECIL** *enters the room. He stands, seemingly stoic.* **CHERYL** *stands.* **LYNN** *enters, silently hysterical.)*

Lynn was eighteen. Nineteen? Eighteen, I was twenty-two. Cecil and I just got engaged.

(**CECIL** *moves toward* **CHERYL**.)

(A moment.)

So what was the ring for? What was the ring for Cecil? Hm?

CECIL. Cheryl I love you.

CHERYL. No. No no no. That is not something you say to me now. You don't get to use those words.

CECIL. Cheryl listen now. I made a mistake this was not –

CHERYL. A mistake? Which part? The sex? Or the knocking up my little sister? Or the engagement? Maybe all three?

CECIL. I want to spend the rest of my life with you.

(He moves toward CHERYL.)

CHERYL. Man I know I can't hurt you physically but if you come any closer.

(CECIL stops.)

LYNN. I'm so so sorry. Cheryl it didn't mean anything. We were drinking and // –

CHERYL. If you don't stop talking I just may kill you.

You gonna keep the baby?

LYNN. Umm. I, I, I –

CHERYL. Are you going to keep the child?!

LYNN. I don't know. I don't know.

CHERYL. I do. You are. Of course you are, your spoiled ass always had to have everything I had. Had to do everything I did and it was always my fault whenever you fucked up. // "Why did you let your sister?"

LYNN. That's not my fault! You can't blame me for Mom and Dad // –

CHERYL. It's going to be my fault I hear it already! "You brought that man around her."

LYNN. What do you want me to do?

CHERYL. You selfish bitch.

Oh my god you're going to keep the baby.

LYNN. I, I, I could say that Tony knocked me up. No one has to know.

CHERYL. I know. I know!

CECIL. Cheryl look at me. Girl look at me. I will stop drinking. I'll move to Michigan. I will do whatever you want me to do

CHERYL. Shut up. Just shut your mouth.

I left everything. Everything I knew to move here to Mississippi. Missa-fucking-sippi. What nigga moves TO Mississippi? But my dumb ass is "in love."

CECIL. I'm not making excuses. I messed up big time. We were drunk, it only happened once.

CHERYL. You're always drunk. I'm glad this happened, no I am. Saved me from marrying the town drunk. That's what you are. Stupid. Stupid. Stupid!

CECIL. I'm sorry. I can't lose you.

CHERYL. NOW you can't lose me? Why weren't you worried about losing me before?

CECIL. I'm sorry.

CHERYL. She's pregnant Cecil. My sister. Pregnant by you.

Let. Me. Go.

You make me sick. My parents were right not to trust you. You're a dirty dirty old man. I hope you die a slow painful death.

(CECIL lets go and moves back to behind the wall. LYNN exits. A light change. A breath.)

BRYANT. Aunt Cheryl?

Aunt Cheryl?

CHERYL. Mm?

BRYANT. You okay?

CHERYL. Yeah. Yeah I'm fine baby.

(A moment.)

CHERYL. So ah, as it turned out your mother was pregnant with twins.

BRYANT. Does my father know?

CHERYL. Tony? He always knew. Not that Cecil was your father but he knew you guys were not his. He didn't care. He loved your mother so much he packed her up and moved her with his family in New York.

BRYANT. This is wild. This is is, a lot.

Why'd you stay with...

Why'd you stay?

CHERYL. Love will make you do things you would never dream.

He stopped drinking and was tenacious. God he was a tenacious man. And I, as angry and hurt as I was, I never saw myself being without him. I never really could imagine living the rest of our lives apart. Love is forgiveness and forgiveness is Love.

BRYANT. I think I bought that Hallmark card once.

CHERYL. You have his sense of humor you know?

(A moment.)

BRYANT. Why lie?

CHERYL. Started out as embarrassment. Shame. Then habit.

Once you commit to a lie, the lying becomes easy. Once it's easy the lie becomes an acceptable truth. I'm so sorry Bryant. I know this is so much to deal with, with everything.

BRYANT. Hey if you could live with your sister smashing your man, getting pregnant and then every other summer or spring break watch and help raise us like it's all good...yo I'll be aight.

(He hugs **CHERYL**.*)*

We're gonna be all right. We good.

*(***CHERYL*** melts into the embrace, then hugs* **BRYANT** *back.)*

(A moment.)

Aunt Cheryl.

CHERYL. Mm-hm?

BRYANT. My arm.

CHERYL. Oh! Oh! I'm sorry baby.

(A tension-relief laugh. A breath.)

X.

(**EMORY** *lies asleep on the bed in the middle room.* **LYNN, BRYANT, JAMES,** *and* **CHERYL** *stand around the front room. An awkward silence.*)

LYNN. So do you have any more questions for us?

(*A moment.*)

CHERYL. Anything at all?

BRYANT. Well yeah.

LYNN. Go ahead. Ask.

BRYANT. Okay. This is hard.

CHERYL. Ask away Bry.

BRYANT. Okay. So.

If a train leaves Little Rock at five p.m. traveling at 100 miles per hour and another train leaves...

LYNN. Can't you ever be serious?

CHERYL. James you've been really quiet.

JAMES. No. I'm fine. I'm going to go wait in the car.

LYNN. Um. Okay. Well say goodbye to Bubba we won't be able to swing by again before our flight.

(**JAMES** *exits.*)

BRYANT. Mom let him be. I'm going to go say peace to Em.

(*He walks to the middle room. He watches* **EMORY** *for a moment.*)

Yo, you in here getting your hairy palm Sunday on?

So we're not cousins we're brothers. Bra-usins.

My dude, I had this whole speech I was gonna say to you that I've been rehearsing in my head and I can't remember nothing. I think the Vicodin is scrambling my brain cells.

I, umm. Cousin to brother's an upgrade and I already saw you as my brother so really there's no change.

I love you my dude. As soon as y'all get out to Michigan I'm there. Between my New York swag and your Mississippi swag the girls are gonna go Lady Ga-Ga over us.

> *(He taps the bed. Waits a moment, then walks to the front room. He hugs CHERYL.)*

So you're still my aunt right?

CHERYL. Boy. Bye.

> *(BRYANT exits.)*

LYNN. What am I gonna do with him? With them?

CHERYL. Gotta take it day by day I suppose.

LYNN. I mean they're practically men, it's not like I can put them on punishment anymore.

CHERYL. Just keep trying and trying until you get through. Don't give up.

> *(A moment.)*

LYNN. You gave up.

CHERYL. What do you mean Lynn?

LYNN. On Emory. You gave up.

CHERYL. Please don't start. You guys are about to leave...

LYNN. You gave up. I saw it in your face when Emory was all bloody and again at the hospital. I thought it was shock but it wasn't, was it?

CHERYL. Lynn I'm really tired.

LYNN. Remember what Dad used to say when he'd have a bad day at work? When Mom or we would ask him how his day was, what he'd say.

CHERYL. "I wish I woke up dead."

LYNN. I wish I woke up dead. I used to laugh every time he said it, it was the way he'd say it.

CHERYL. Yeah I remember.

LYNN. And I'd always think, how does someone "wake up dead," if you're dead you don't wake up.

CHERYL. Lynn.

LYNN. When Mom passed and Dad soon after, I got it. I understood how you could wake up dead. When you called to say Cecil had passed I felt the same way and I know you've been feeling like that like you've been waking up dead for months now.

CHERYL. Lynn.

LYNN. I never told you this, ashamed to admit it I guess, but one of the reasons I told myself – to make sleeping with Cecil okay – was that I was doing it for you. Thought if you found out you'd realize he was no good for you. Did it for you, the stories we tell ourselves.

You can't give up. I can't... I can't handle healing all these wounds by myself, you probably could but I can't. I need you. You forgave me and I don't think I could've forgiven myself but you did and I knew this funeral would bring up old wounds and maybe new ones but I wasn't worried. I wasn't worried because no matter what I knew you'd see us through this but you're becoming hard. Don't. Don't. It's not you. If you do the boys might not ever heal from this because I can't heal it. But you can. I know it's not fair to put it all on you but it's true. It's true.

(A minute.)

(She hugs **CHERYL** *[it's the first time they've touched the entire weekend].)*

Don't become hard. Okay?

Okay.

(She exits. Outside, the sound of a car-door slam.)

(A moment.)

*(**JAMES** enters. He walks to **CHERYL**, hugs and kisses her.)*

JAMES. I'm going to say bye to Emory.

CHERYL. Okay baby. Take your time.

*(She sees Bryant's pill bottle, picks it up, and walks out. **JAMES** walks to the back room.)*

JAMES. Hey.

*(**EMORY** rolls over and stares at **JAMES**.)*

EMORY. What James?

JAMES. I just wanted to say. Um.

EMORY. Daddy used to call you the weak twin.

JAMES. What?

EMORY. He used to call you the weak twin, that's why he gave you that knife.

JAMES. Emory I just came in here to say // –

EMORY. "Bryant's strong he can handle himself but that James, can't have him walking around without some sort of protection."

JAMES. Goodbye Emory.

EMORY. Called you the weak twin. You were a disappointment. We're both disappointments. At least I'm crazy. What's your excuse? Maybe you are crazy. We are brothers. Crazy just like me. Crazy worthless nigger.

> *(He laughs. **JAMES** charges at him, grabs a pillow, and starts pummeling him with it. **EMORY** continues to laugh. Before **EMORY** can defend himself, **JAMES** is on top of him, smothering him with the pillow. The room pulsates with the low lub-dub of a heartbeat. A tinny, high-pitched tone swells and fills the room. **CHERYL** enters the house.)*

CHERYL. James your mother's ready to go.

> *(She enters the middle room and immediately pulls **JAMES** off of **EMORY**. The sounds cease.)*

Stop it! Are you crazy?!

> *(**JAMES** begins to weep. **EMORY** is still.)*

Emory baby?

> *(She checks **EMORY**'s body. Seeing that he's not breathing, **CHERYL** performs mouth to mouth. **EMORY** doesn't respond.)*

Oh my god.

> *(**BRYANT** enters the house.)*

BRYANT. Yo! Let's go man.

CHERYL. He'll be right there!

James, James, look at me. This will be our secret okay? Okay?

JAMES. I'm sorry.

CHERYL. It's okay. It was an accident. Go home. Go with your brother. I'll take care of Emory.

JAMES. Aunt Cher– //

> (**CHERYL** *slaps* **JAMES.**)

CHERYL. Go damn you.

> (*She hugs him.*)

I love you. It was an accident. Go home.

BRYANT. Jay!

CHERYL. Go now go.

> (**JAMES** *hugs* **CHERYL** *again. Then walks to the front.*)

BRYANT. Are those tears? I knew you really loved that kid. Come on punk. Bye again! For real this time!

> (**BRYANT** *and* **JAMES** *exit.* **CHERYL** *lies down next to* **EMORY.** *Watches him for a moment. A minute. A breath.*)

CHERYL. We'll sleep now. Okay baby? Sleep now and figure it all out in the morning. Figure it all out when we wake up.

> (*Lights fade.*)

End of Play

www.ingramcontent.com/pod-product-compliance
Lightning Source LLC
Chambersburg PA
CBHW051409290426
44108CB00015B/2221